The Naked Octopus

The Naked Octopus

Erotic haiku in English
with Japanese translations

By
Gabriel Rosenstock

Translated by
Mariko Sumikura

Illustrated by
Mathew Staunton

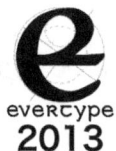

evertype
2013

Published by Evertype, Cnoc Sceichín, Leac an Anfa, Cathair na Mart, Co. Mhaigh Eo, Éire. www.evertype.com.

Text © 2013 Gabriel Rosenstock.
Japanese translation © 2013 Mariko Sumikura.
Illustrations © 2013 Mathew Staunton.

All rights reserved. No part of this publication may be reproduced, stored in a retrieval system, or transmitted, in any form or by any means, electronic, mechanical, photocopying, recording, or otherwise, without the prior permission in writing of the Publisher, or as expressly permitted by law, or under terms agreed with the appropriate reprographics rights organization.

A catalogue record for this book is available from the British Library.

ISBN-10 1-78201-048-3
ISBN-13 978-1-78201-048-7

Typeset in Hiragino Kaku Gothic Pro W3 (ヒラギノ角ゴ Pro W3) and Hiragino Kaku Gothic Pro W6 (ヒラギノ角ゴ Pro W6) by Mathew Staunton.

Designed and edited by Mathew Staunton.

Cover: Mathew Staunton.

Printed by LightningSource.

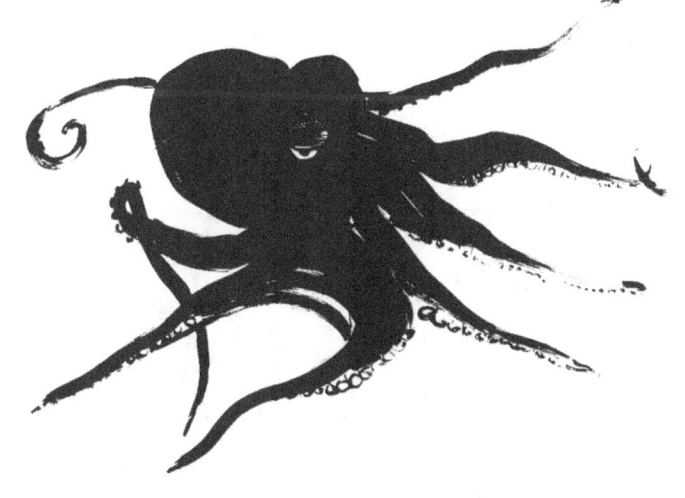

for aeons
I have danced for you silently
on the ocean floor

永劫に
君に踊ろう
洋上の床

here I am at last
naked on the shore—
frozen moon

最後には
浜で裸身に――
凍り月

frustrated by mermaids
I came on land
to find you

人魚消え
陸に上がりて
君に逢う

うねる腕
君をさぐれば
風香る

my tentacles
probing the wind
in search of your scent

'you taste of seaweed'
you say
licking me

藻を食んで
鞭を打ってと
君はいい

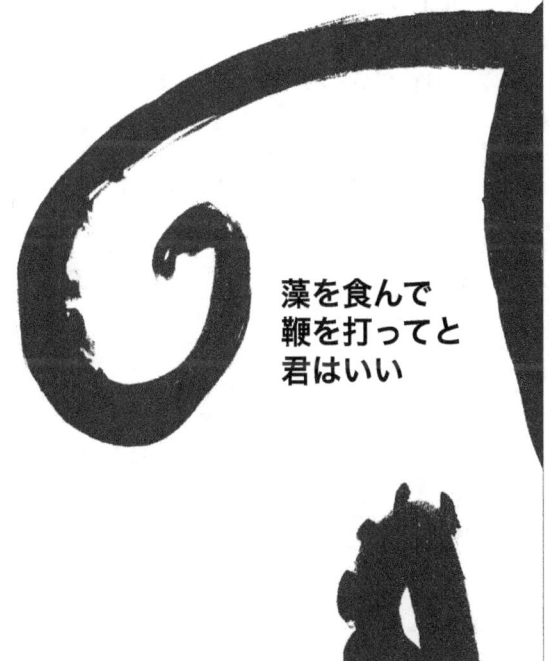

octopus pianist
my love
why do I only play black keys?

ピアノ弾き蛸
黒鍵だけの曲
何故か弾く

octopus firefly-catcher—
something is flickering
under your dress

蛍狩り
点滅する裾
潜り獲る

octopus buddha
please, please
show me some compassion!

仏陀蛸
どうかお願い
慈悲見せて

octopus weather-announcer
my love—
another storm?

予報蛸
またもう一度
嵐かも

octopus astronomer
every night
I discover a new you!

天文学蛸
夜毎見出す
君 新星!

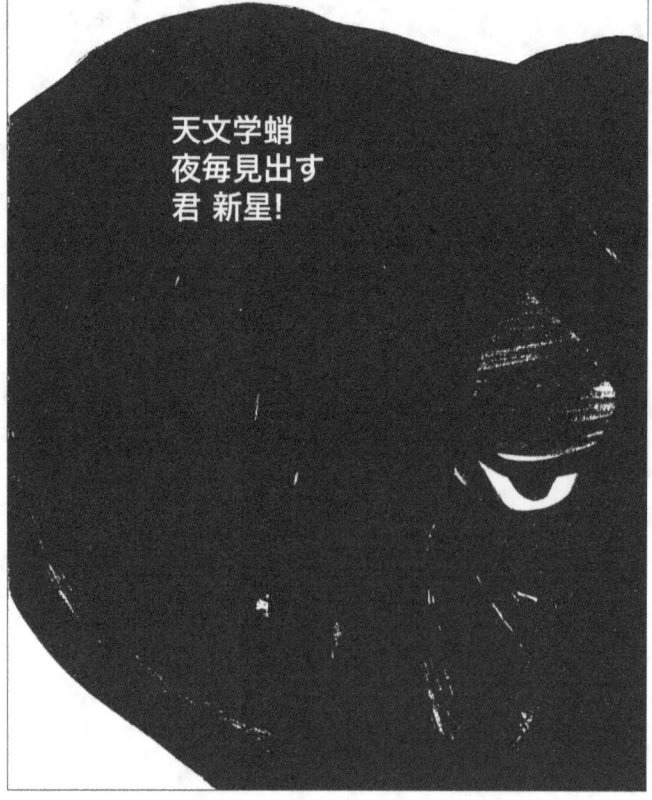

octopus mystery—
who can know
my eight arms?

推理作家
わが手八丁
誰が知る

octopus policeman
I arrest you
for not loving me!

蛸警官
愛さぬときは
君逮捕

奇人蛸
乳首の硬さに
狂い舞う

octopus lunatic
the stiffening of a nipple
drove me insane

octopus drummer—
I play to the rhythm
of your heart

蛸ドラマー
君のリズムに
みだれ打ち

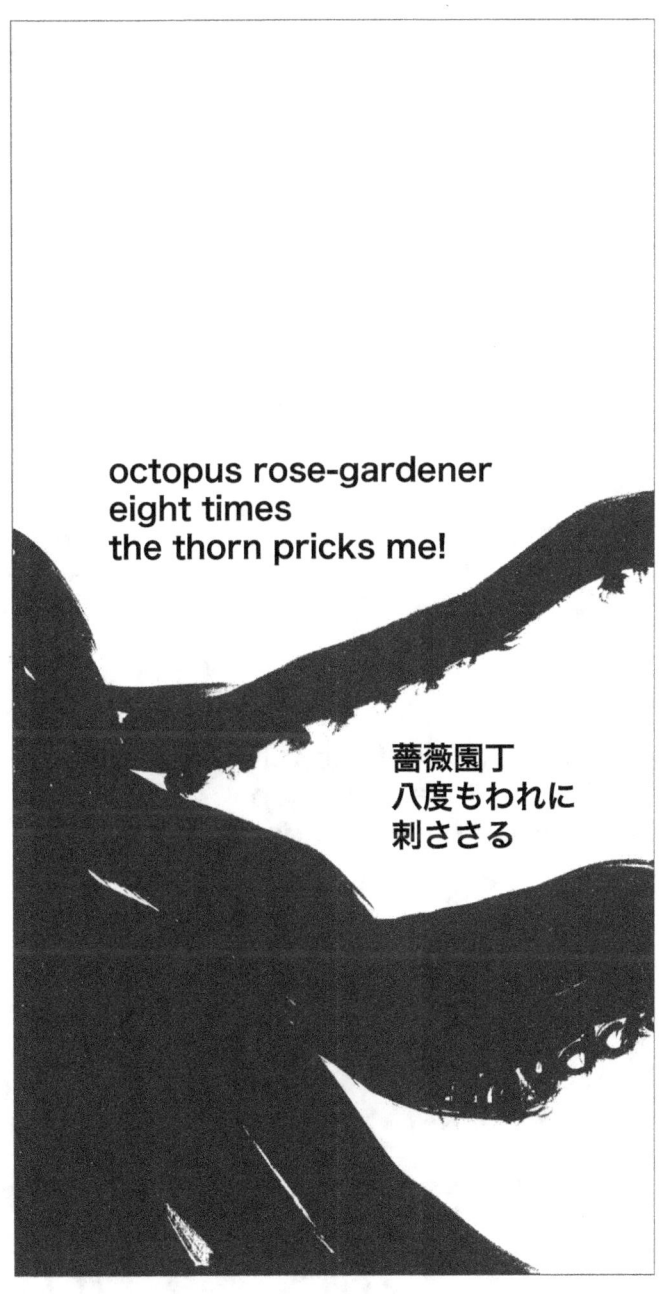

octopus rose-gardener
eight times
the thorn pricks me!

薔薇園丁
八度もわれに
刺ささる

octopus fortune teller—
tonight we will sleep
between satin sheets!

占い蛸
今宵の共寝は
繻子のうえ

octopus street cleaner—
picking up the poems
you have thrown away!

清掃業蛸
君捨てし詩
拾うなり

octopus man in the moon
let me in
through your window

月に住む
蛸男なり
窓開けよ

蛸 力士
八夜 八晩
夢相撲

octopus sumo wrestler
I wrestle each night with
erotic dreams

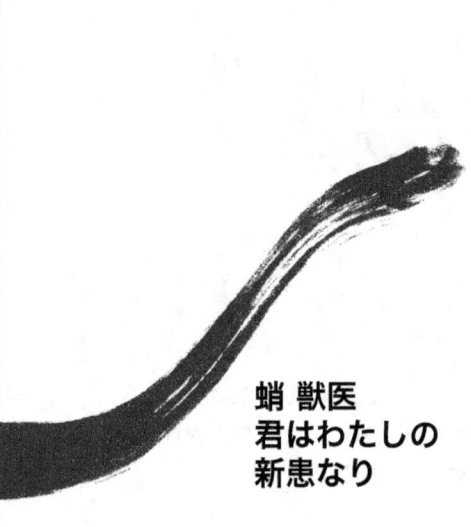

蛸 獣医
君はわたしの
新患なり

octopus vet—
my love
I think you are an animal

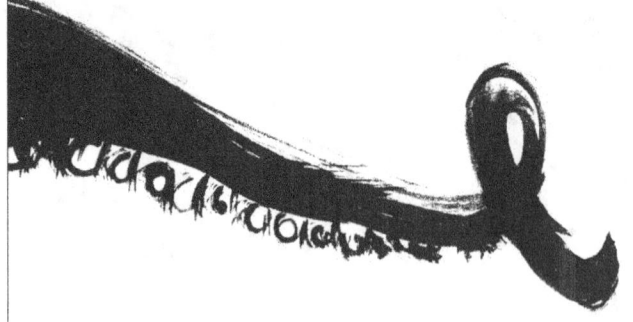

octopus juggler
my heart
I juggle for you!

曲芸蛸
君を手玉に
もてあそぶ

octopus cardiologist—
oh love!
have you no heart?

心臓医
おや 君ないの!
心臓が

混浴で
一箇所のぞき
下肢柔ら

in the hot tub together
all my limbs have grown soft—
except for one

wild dogs bark
in the awful night—
my tentacles surround you

野犬吼ゆ
怖い夜通し
掻き抱く

octopus priest—
I salivate
listening to your confession

司祭蛸
悩み聴きつつ
涎垂れ

octopus flâneur
where are you?
I slither up the lanes of Kyoto

迷い蛸
京の路地這い
君探す

before entering
I clothe my tentacles
in moonlight

入る前
蛸足隠す
月の下

octopus yogi
I stand for you
on one tentacle

ヨガ蛸は
一本足よ
君の前

ぐるぐると
君 われ 夢の
蛸踊り

round and round I spin
dreaming you are mine—
octopus dervish

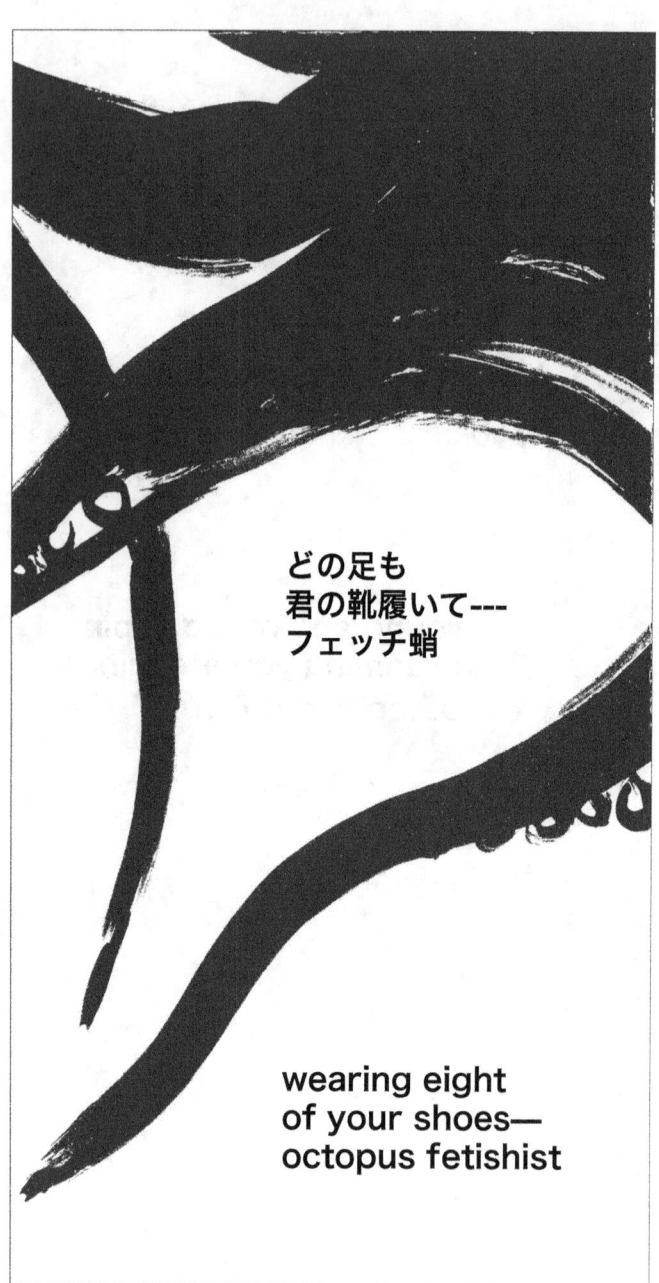

どの足も
君の靴履いて---
フェッチ蛸

wearing eight
of your shoes—
octopus fetishist

nothing under my kilt
but music—
octopus bagpiper

キルト下
楽音だけなり
　（バグ）パイプ吹き

what might our offspring do?
take to the land? the sea?
shimmering stars

子ら如何に
陸にか海か
光る星

手品師蛸
われ消えてゆく
君のなか

octopus magician
I disappear
in you

we wrestle—
what is it we seek?
the dawn? exhaustion

取っ組みて
何探すのか
朝、疲労

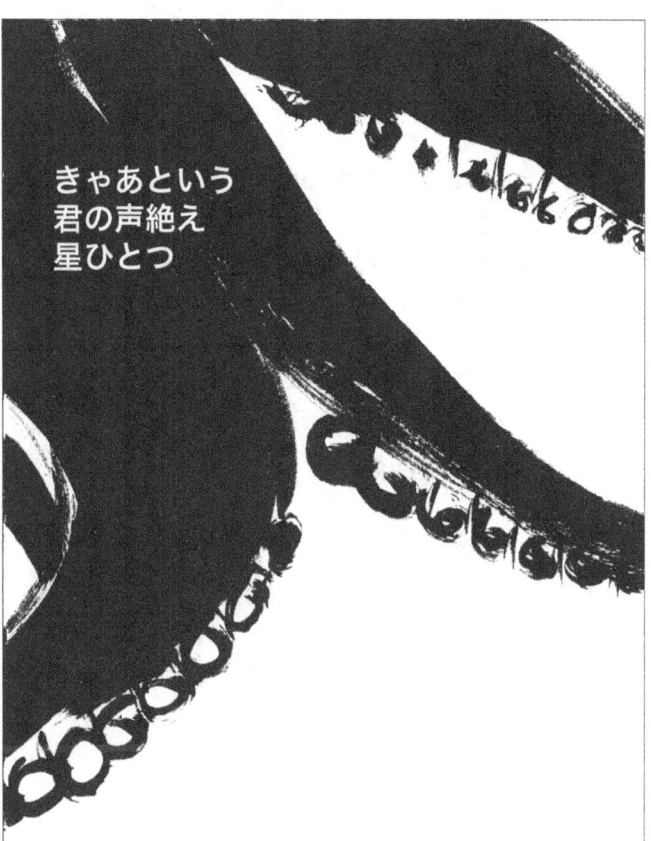

きゃあという
君の声絶え
星ひとつ

when you scream
and when your voice dies in me—
evening star

where is the dawn?
all night I thrust
into your mystery

朝は何処？
夜通し突進
妙なる君へ

look how it rises
your nipple—oh!
Mt Fuji

見よ乳首
盛上がりたり
富士山か

言葉なら
拍車をかけて
陰核へ

these words—spurts of ink—
are shaped
for your clitoris

ほとばしる
君へ　銀河は
消え失せて

spurting into you—
the Milky Way
vanishes

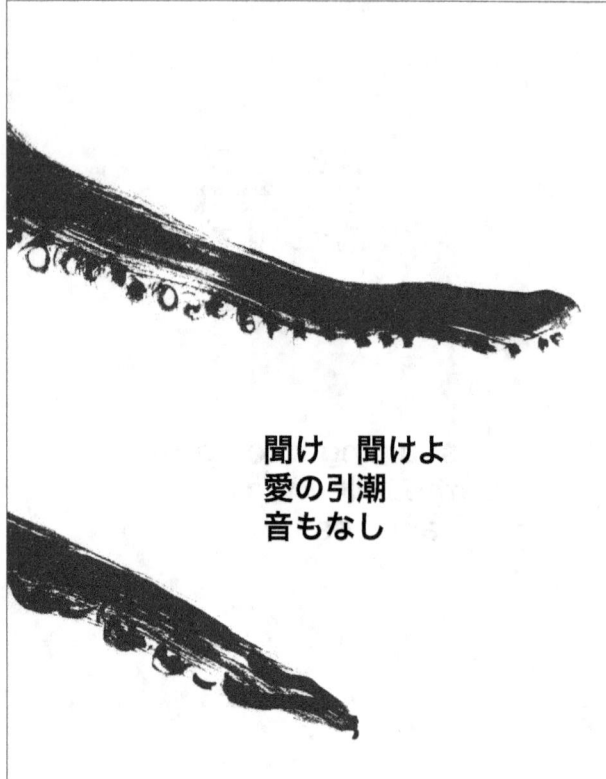

聞け　聞けよ
愛の引潮
音もなし

listen! listen!
the ebbing of our love
has no sound

眠気追い
また愛し合う
秋の虫

goading us to wake up
and make love again—
singing insects

look! it is dawn!
let us roll together
in morning dew

見よ、夜明け
我らもんどり
朝露に

octopus pearl-diver
show me—
reveal your pearl!

蛸の海士（あま）
君の真珠（たま）を
見せたまえ

it's you I touch
you I feel with each string—
octopus harpist

これが君
弦の官能
ハープ奏者

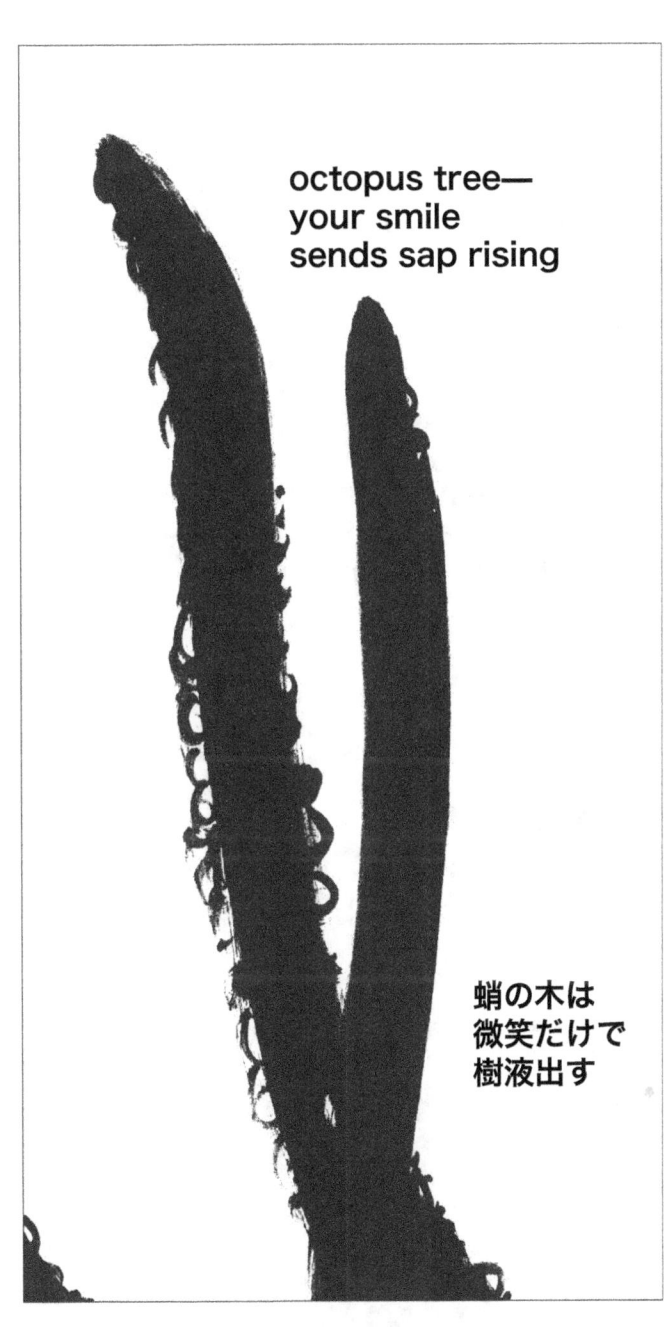

octopus tree—
your smile
sends sap rising

蛸の木は
微笑だけで
樹液出す

I will name them all
those stars in your eyes—
octopus astronomer

名付けたし
君の目の星
天文学蛸

octopus philosopher—
what was I
before you?

哲学蛸
われなりしかと
君の前

メディア蛸
いつも君が
大見出し

octopus journalist
you are always
in my headlines

溶接工　蛸
くっつく夢を
見てばかり

octopus welder—
I dream
of our union

octopus politician—
sweetest darling, yes!
I accept your bribe

政治蛸ー
君の賄賂は
ありがたく

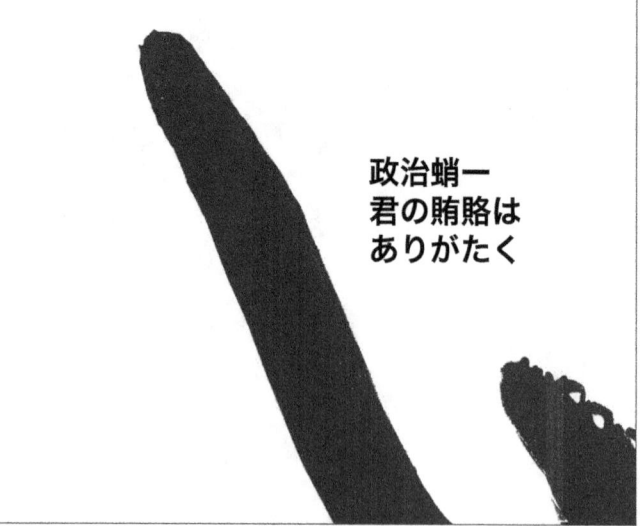

octopus geometrician—
I am very interested
in your curves

君の曲線（カーブ）
好奇尽きない
幾何学蛸

shining nipples
reflected now
in my sad eyes

光る乳首
慕うわが眼に
涙あり

then I opened your bag
and stole your lipstick—
octopus mugger

君のポーチ
開け紅（べに）盗るや
蛸強盗

I hide atop an old pine tree
you gaze through me
at the full moon

松が枝の
僕を通して
月をみる

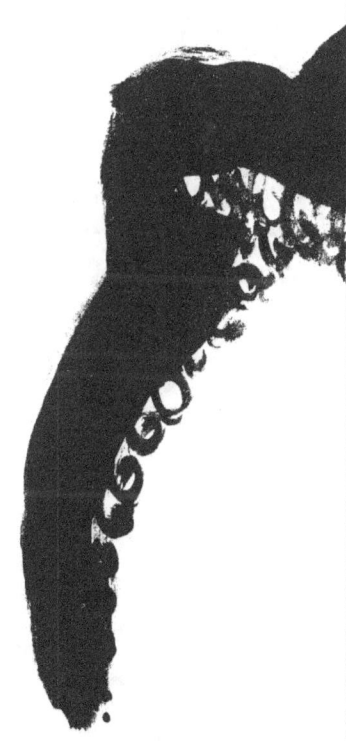

lost I was
completely lost
until you lost yourself in me

ぐったりだ
君もぐったり
僕のなか

my lust is for you
and for the sea—
are we not one?

君ま欲し
海ま欲しとや---
我ら一体

why do they interrupt
our love making?
pine crickets

邪魔するな
僕らの恋路
松小虫

octopus fire-eater
I breathe the flame
of your being

火食い蛸
炎吹き込む
君のなか

octopus explorer—
show me, love—
where have I not been?

蛸　探検者
知らないところ
見に行こう

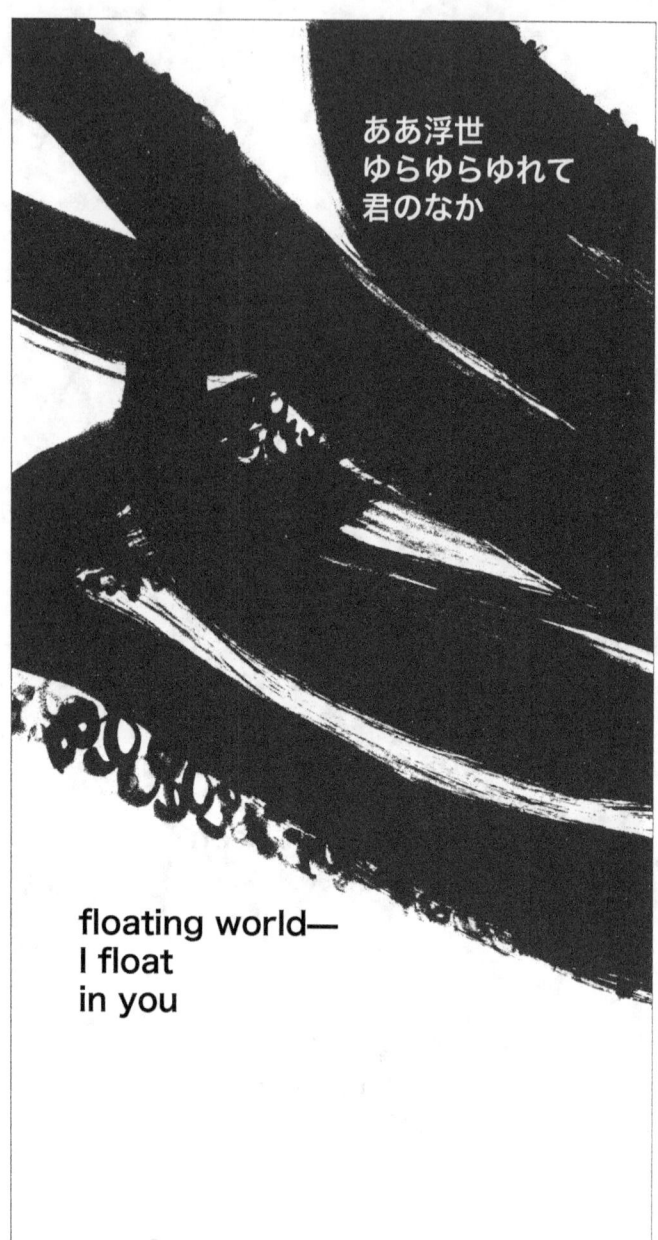

ああ浮世
ゆらゆらゆれて
君のなか

floating world—
I float
in you

落柿舎で
朝まで君と
熟し柿

let us enter Kyorai's hut—
I will feed you crushed persimmons
till dawn

octopus tango—
are you in me
or am I in you?

タンゴ蛸
きみ僕のなか
僕きみのなか?

how lovely you are
when you turn blue—
are my tentacles choking you?

愛しくて
蛸足締めれば
仮死の君

licking your tears away
I hear the distant salty sound
of home

涙甜め
遠い潮騒
故里(くに)想う

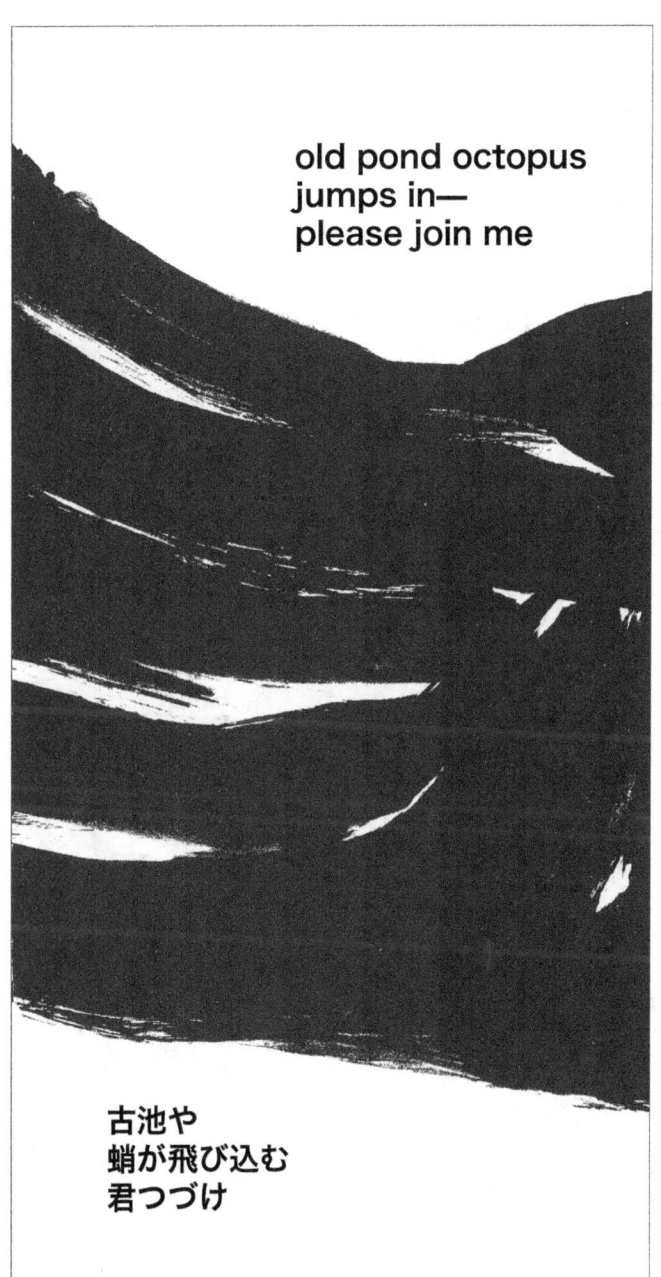

old pond octopus
jumps in—
please join me

古池や
蛸が飛び込む
君つづけ

you have left—
who can hear my tentacles cry?
Shakuhachi

君往けばーー
蛸足 尺八
啼く音聞け

frosty morning—
a deer licks another—
as I licked you

霜の朝---
鹿舐め合うように
君舐める

octopus kite-flyer that's
my heart up there—
flying for you

蛸の風
高う高うあがれ
君揚がれ

カラオケや
虫の音鳴くや
君のなか

karaoke
of singing insects
as I penetrate you

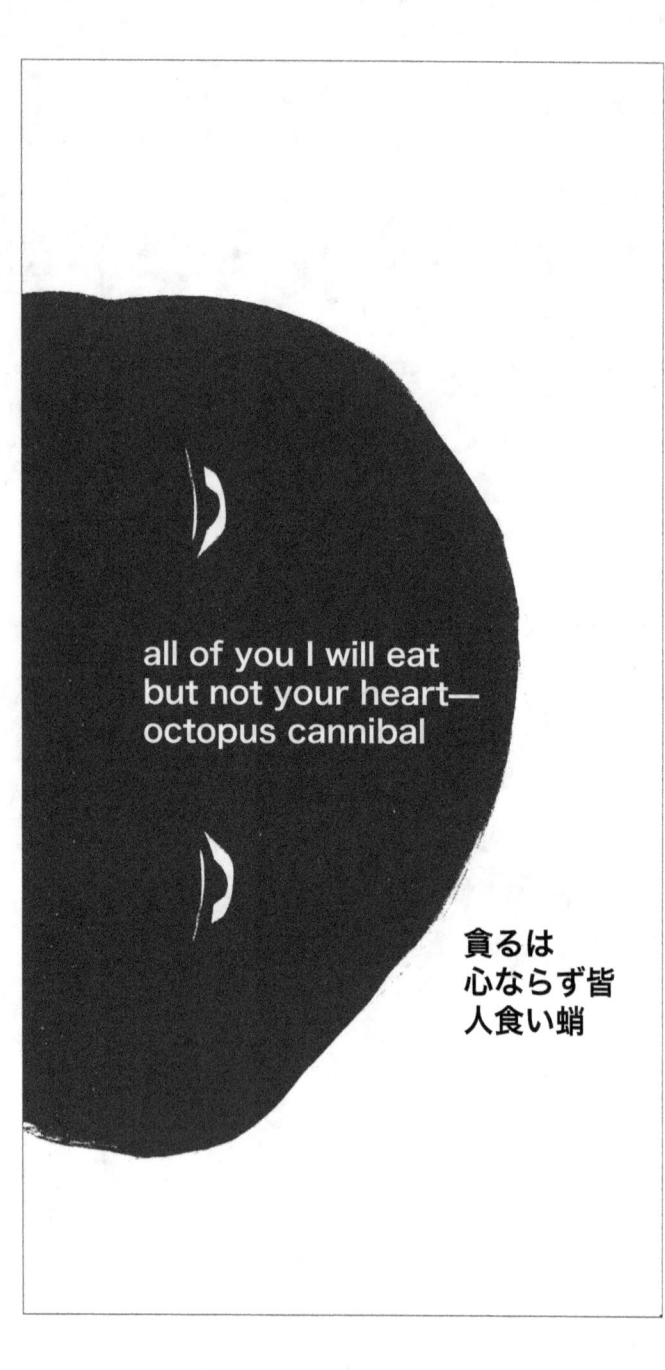

my song is you
and the silence afterwards—
octopus boatman

歌は君
後の静けさ
蛸水夫

one glance from you
and the bamboo stiffens—
octopus gardener

君ちらり
竹強ばりて
造園家蛸

the narrow road
to your deep north—
widening

狭き道
深き北方
広くする

now you know
why I have lingered on this earth—
octopus bodhisattva

君知りぬ
縁深き理由(わけ)
蛸菩薩

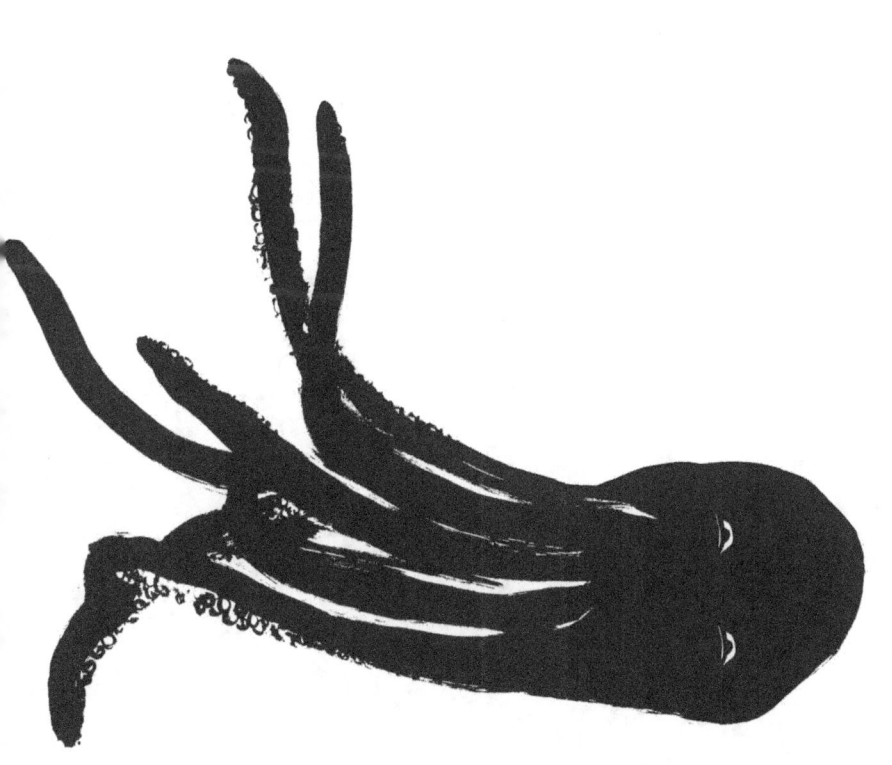

www.ingramcontent.com/pod-product-compliance
Lightning Source LLC
Chambersburg PA
CBHW071420220526
45469CB00004B/1356